Mommy's Giant Melons

By: Mama JC

Illustrations by: Gustyawan

This book is dedicated to **my mother** who so graciously passed her giant melons on to her daughter. Thank you for putting up with me.
I love you.

FIRST EDITION

www.mamajc.com

I went to the store with my mommy today, and a gentleman stopped her along the way.

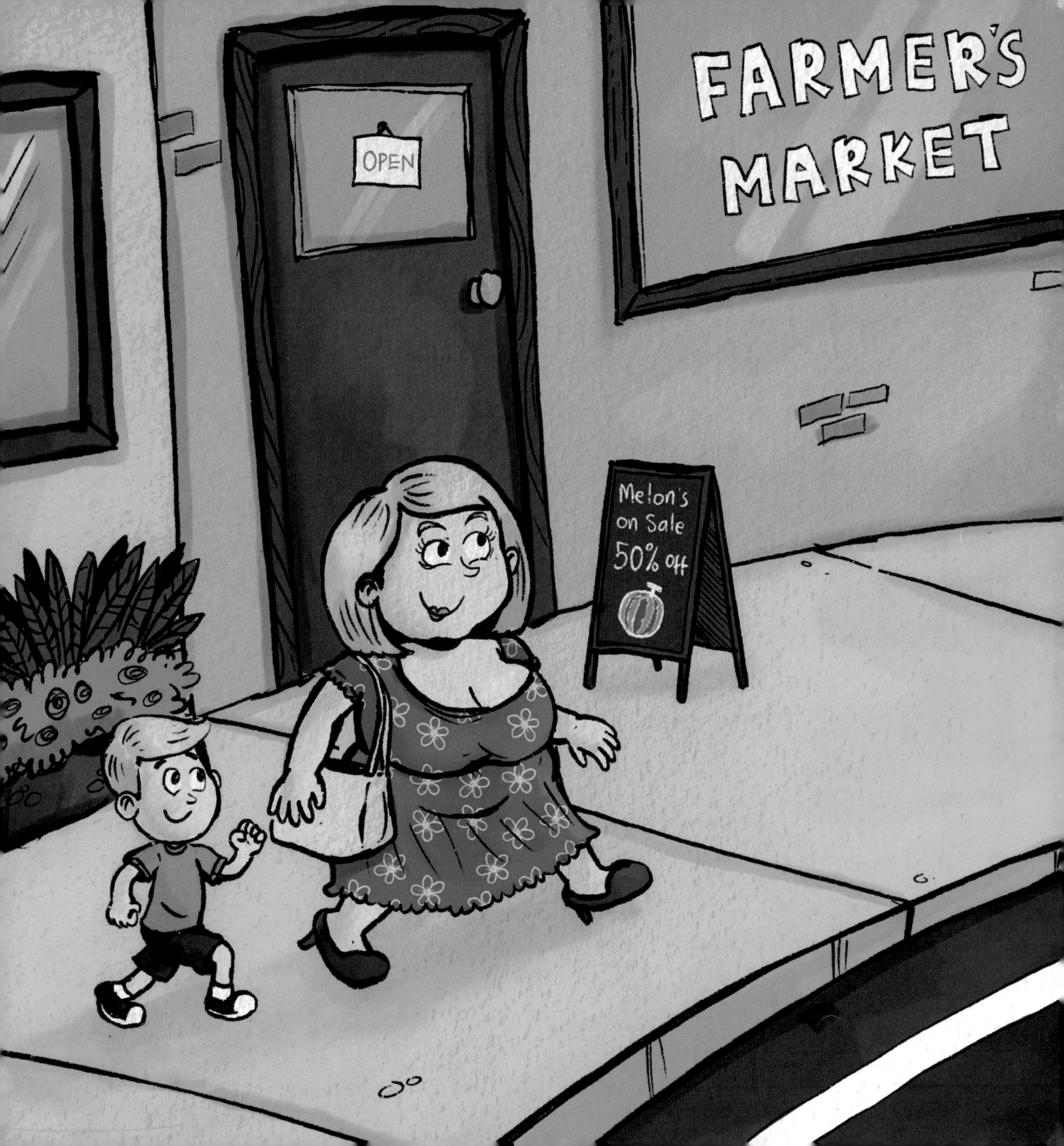

OPEN
FARMER'S MARKET
Melon's on Sale 50% off

"Excuse me Missus, I can't help but stare...
Those melons are the largest I've seen
anywhere."

"Thank you good sir, I am glad you
approve, but staring you see is incredibly
rude."

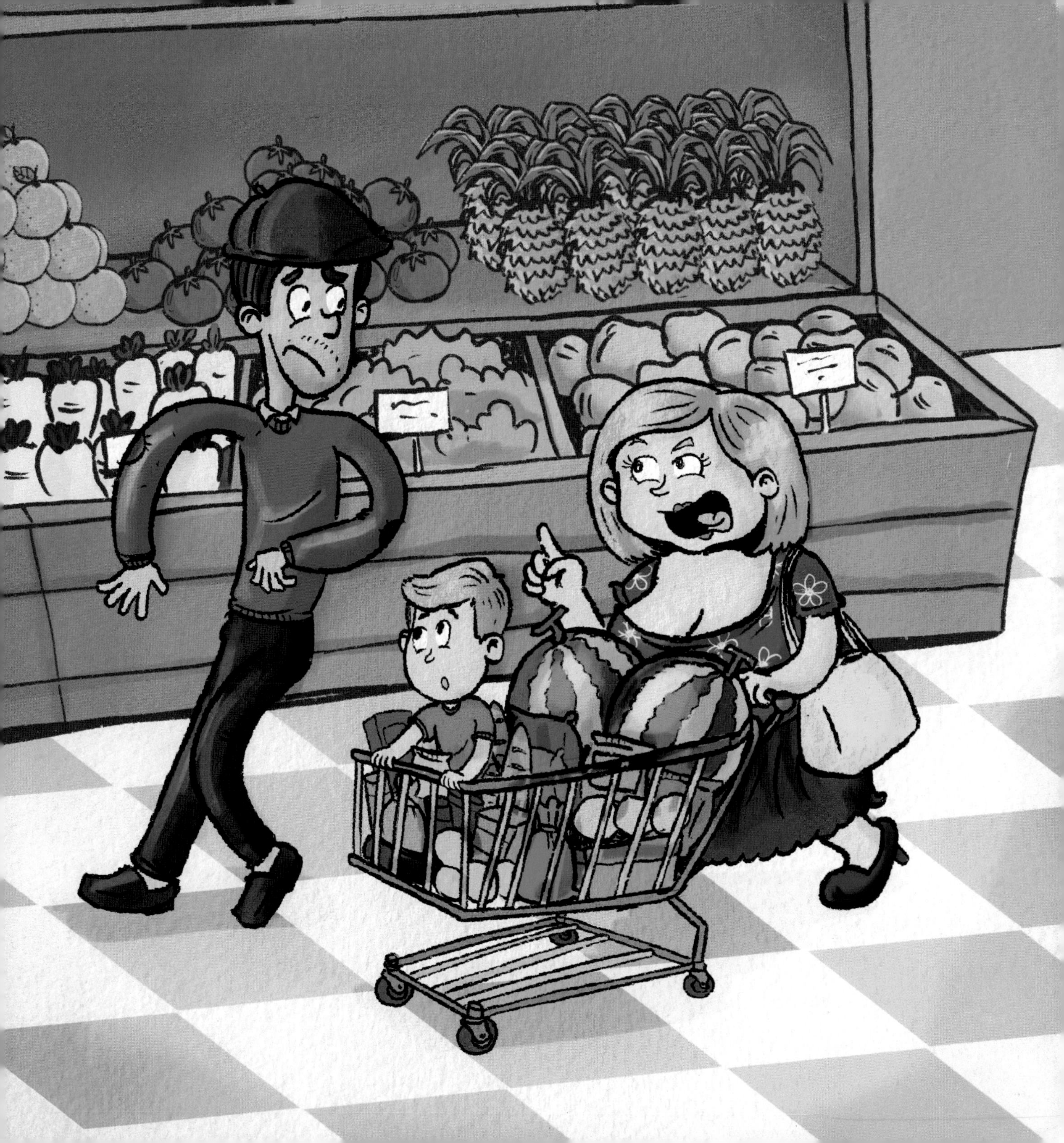

Her melons were HUGE; you couldn't imagine, like Mars in the sky or eggs from a dragon.

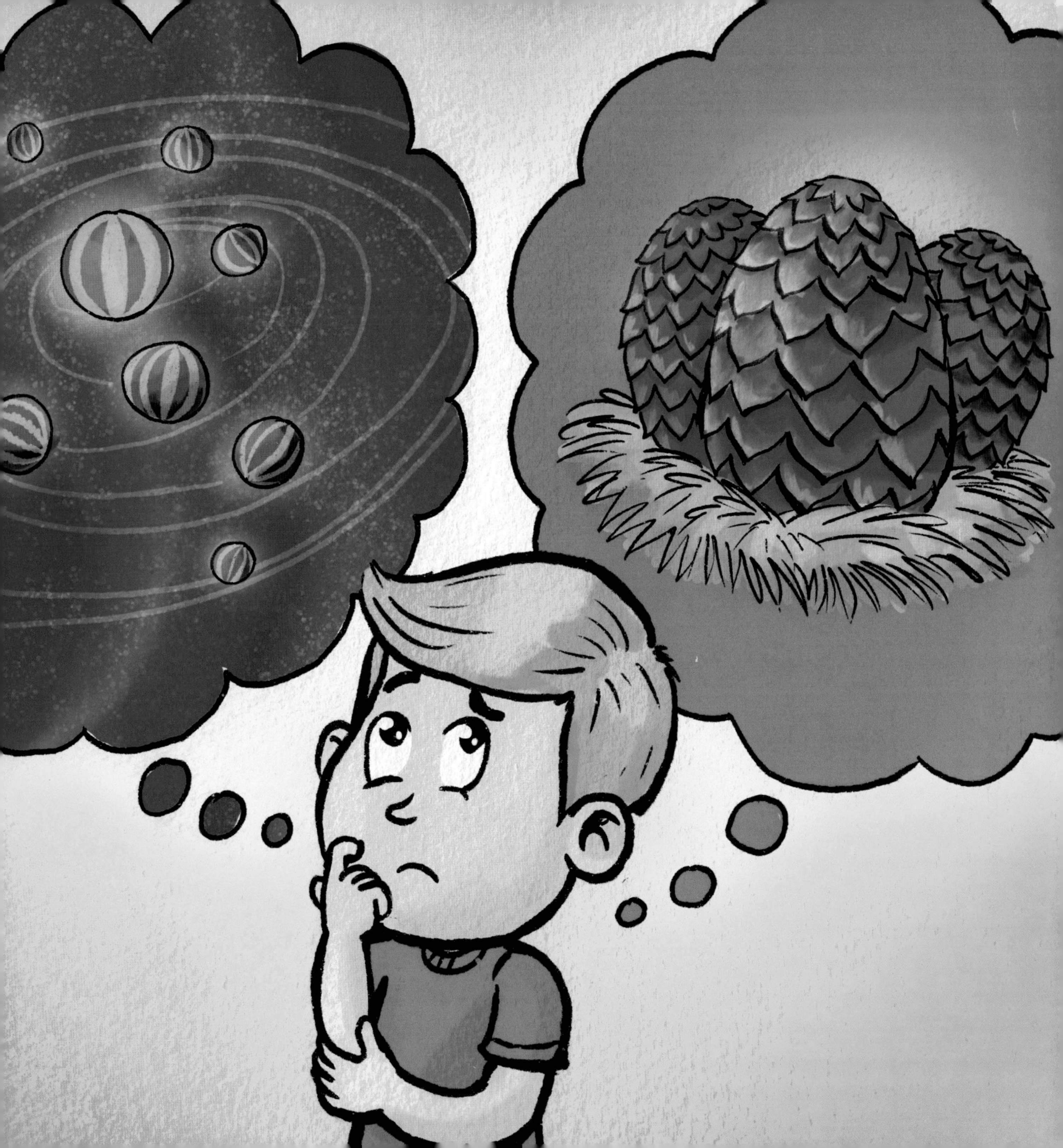

The melons were thrown in a sack round her shoulders. At a distance they looked like a couple of boulders.

But even despite a strong double bag, before we could leave they had started to sag.

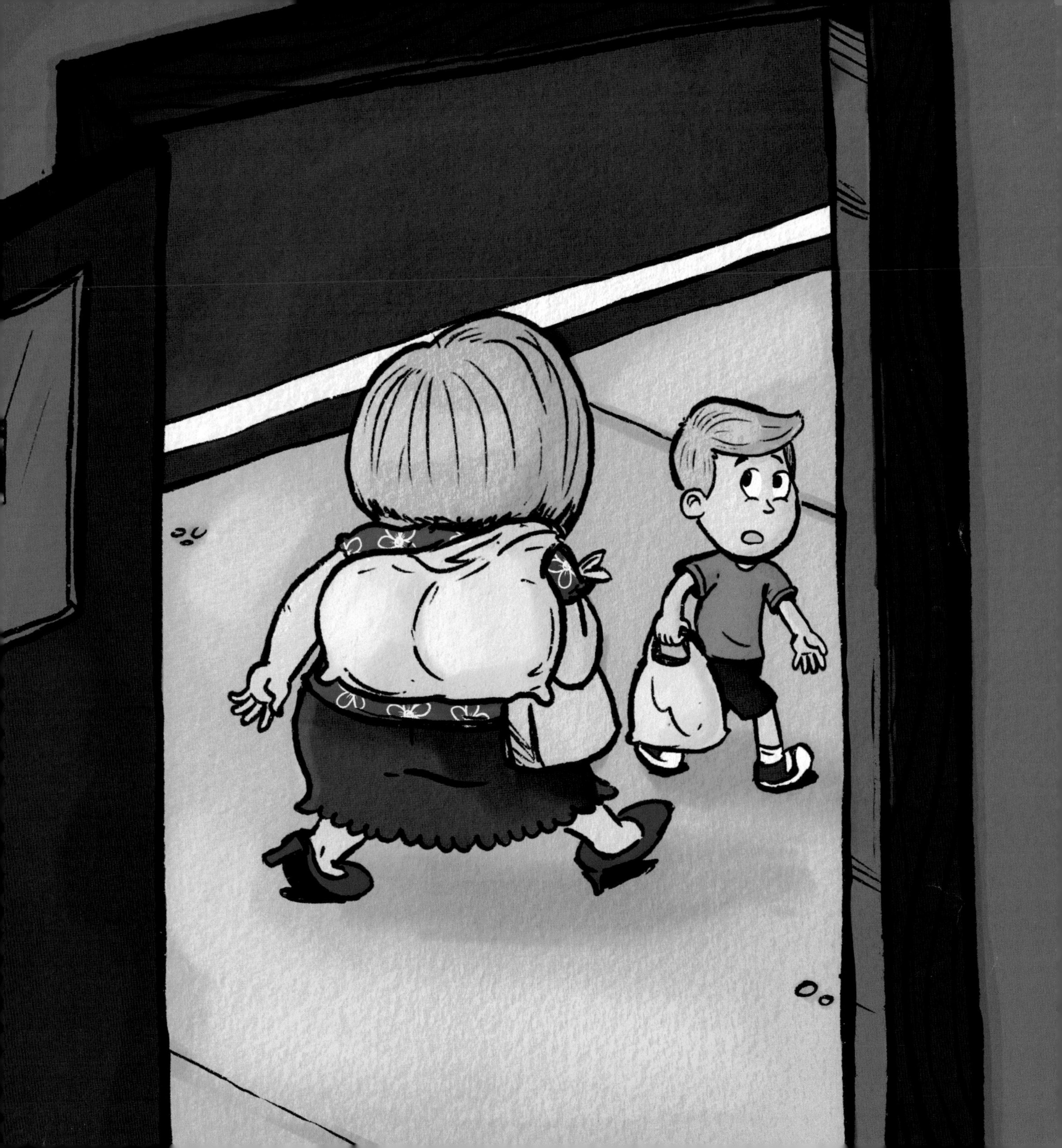

So wrapped in a shirt we were off for a stroll through Central Park - a melon patrol.

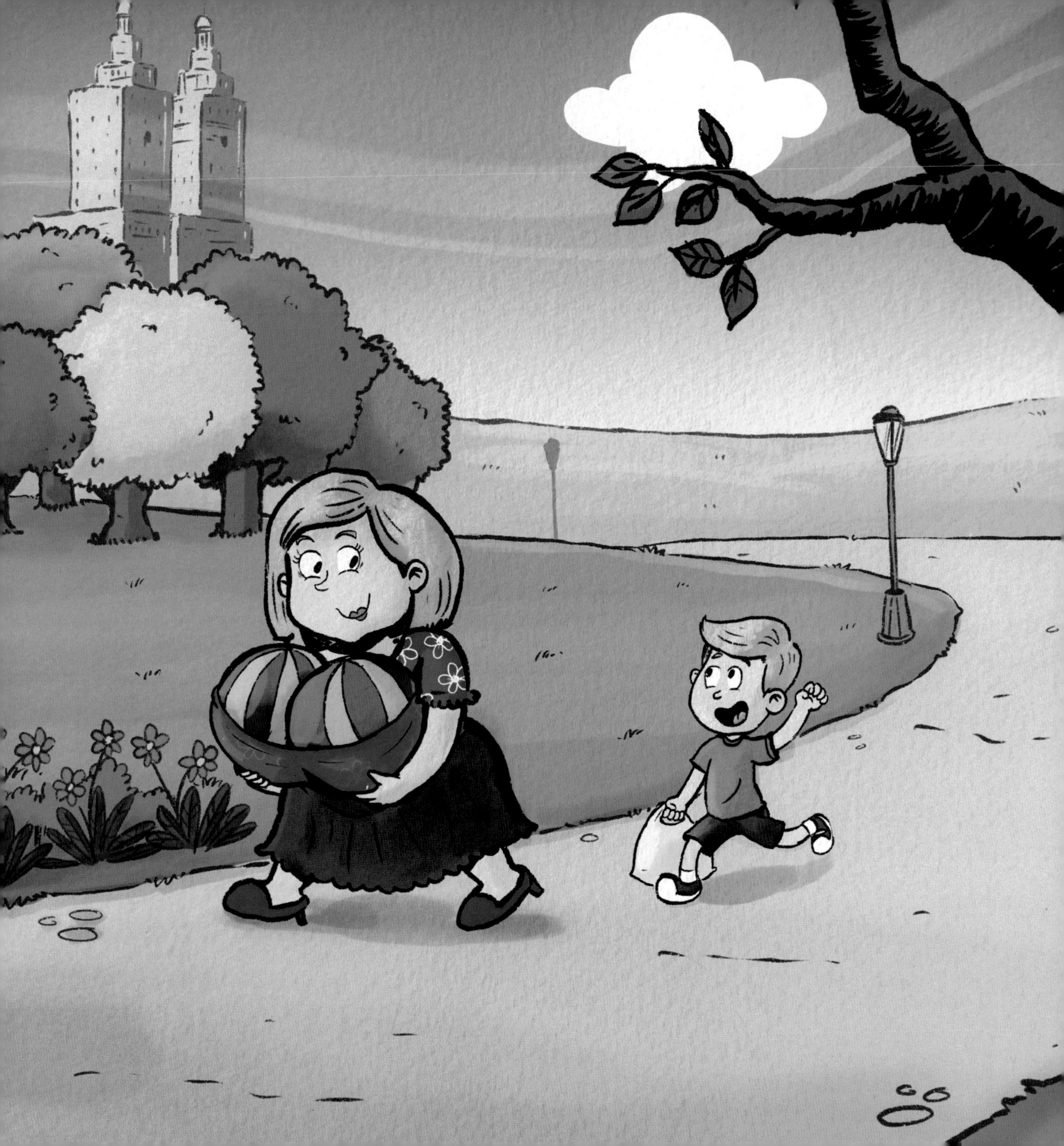

Some were in shock, while some simply gazed at the monstrous melons, they were truly amazed.

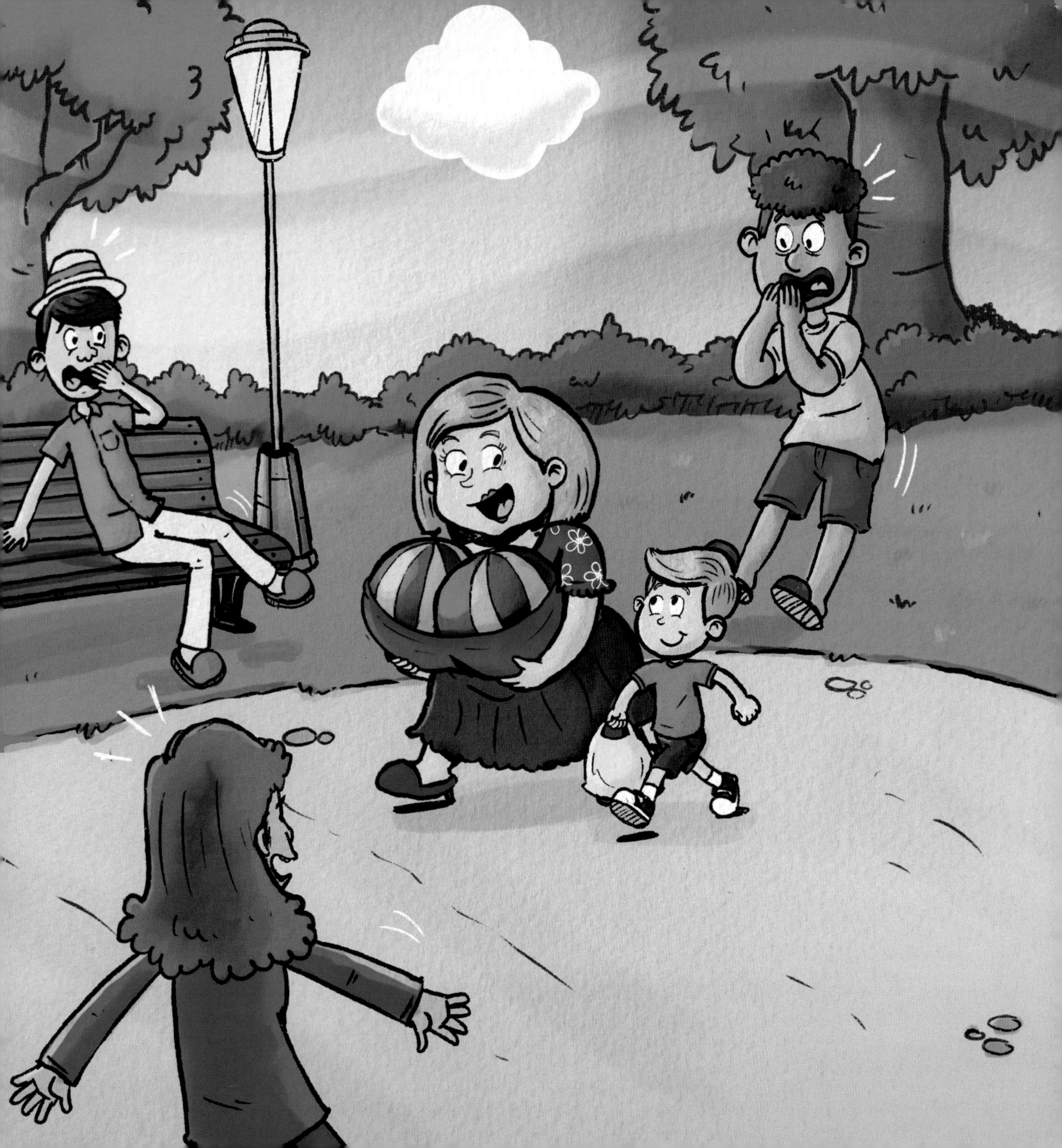

"Hey there Betty, do think you could share? It looks like you've plenty of melons to spare."

"Aren't they both great?!" I'd share if I could, but these are for hubby. Get some; they're good.

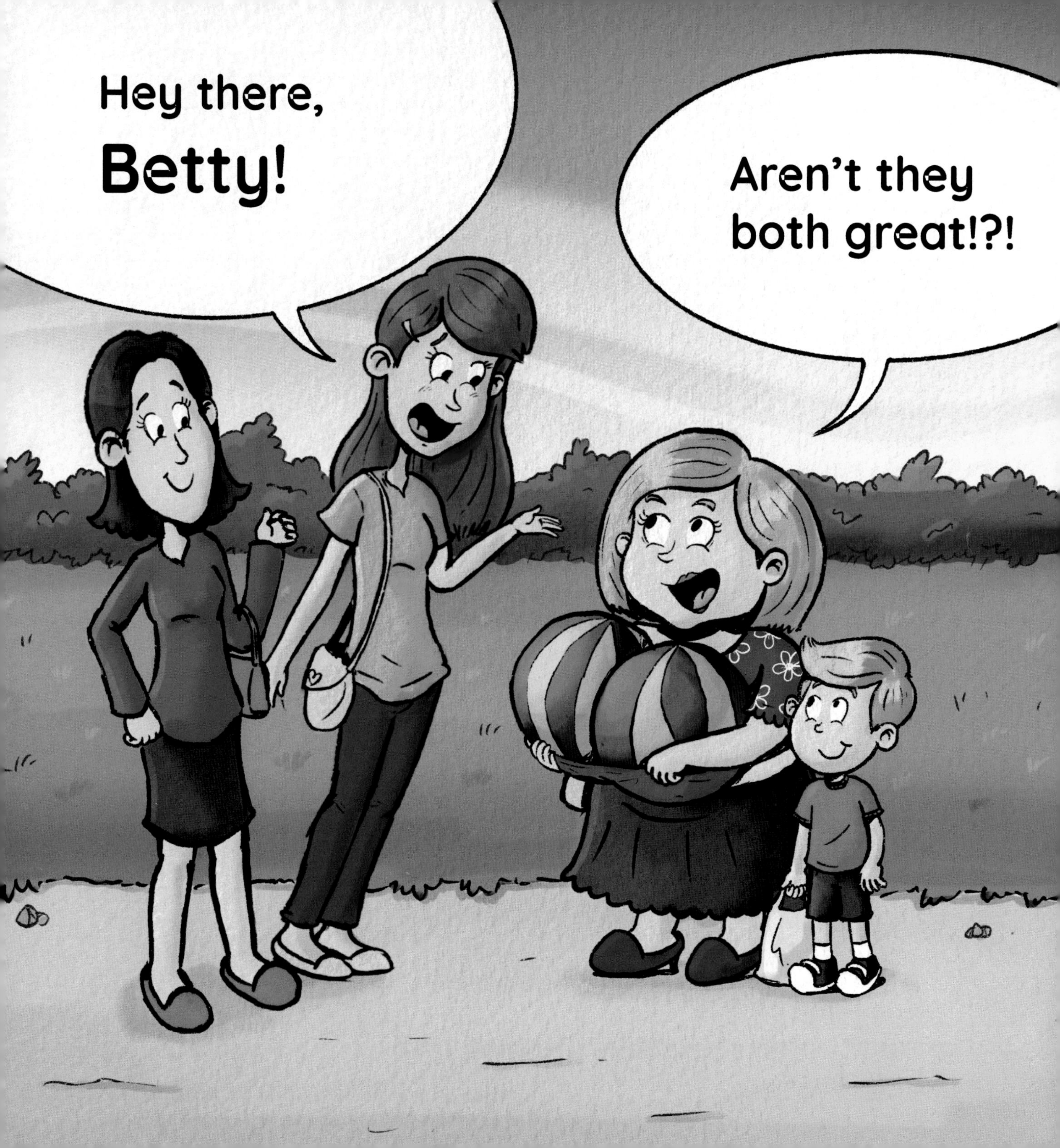
Hey there, Betty!
Aren't they both great!?!

"When they handed out melons - all we could find were the size of a lemon and that would be kind."

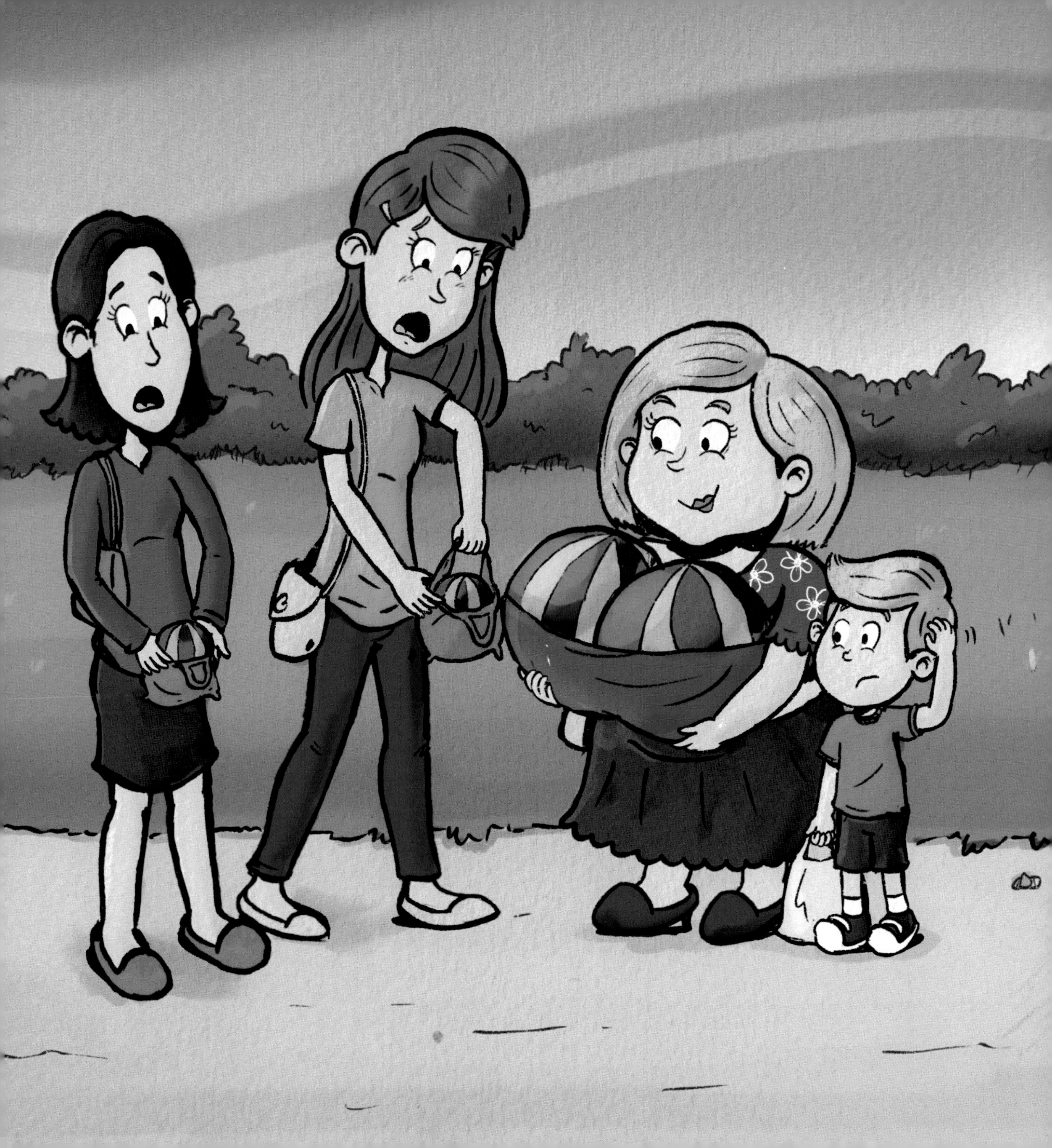

"It's ok ladies, you can always get more,
Dr. Michaels sells melons, you know, by the
score."

"Dr. Michaels sells melons? I wouldn't have
guessed" "He helped me get mine, his
place is the best!"

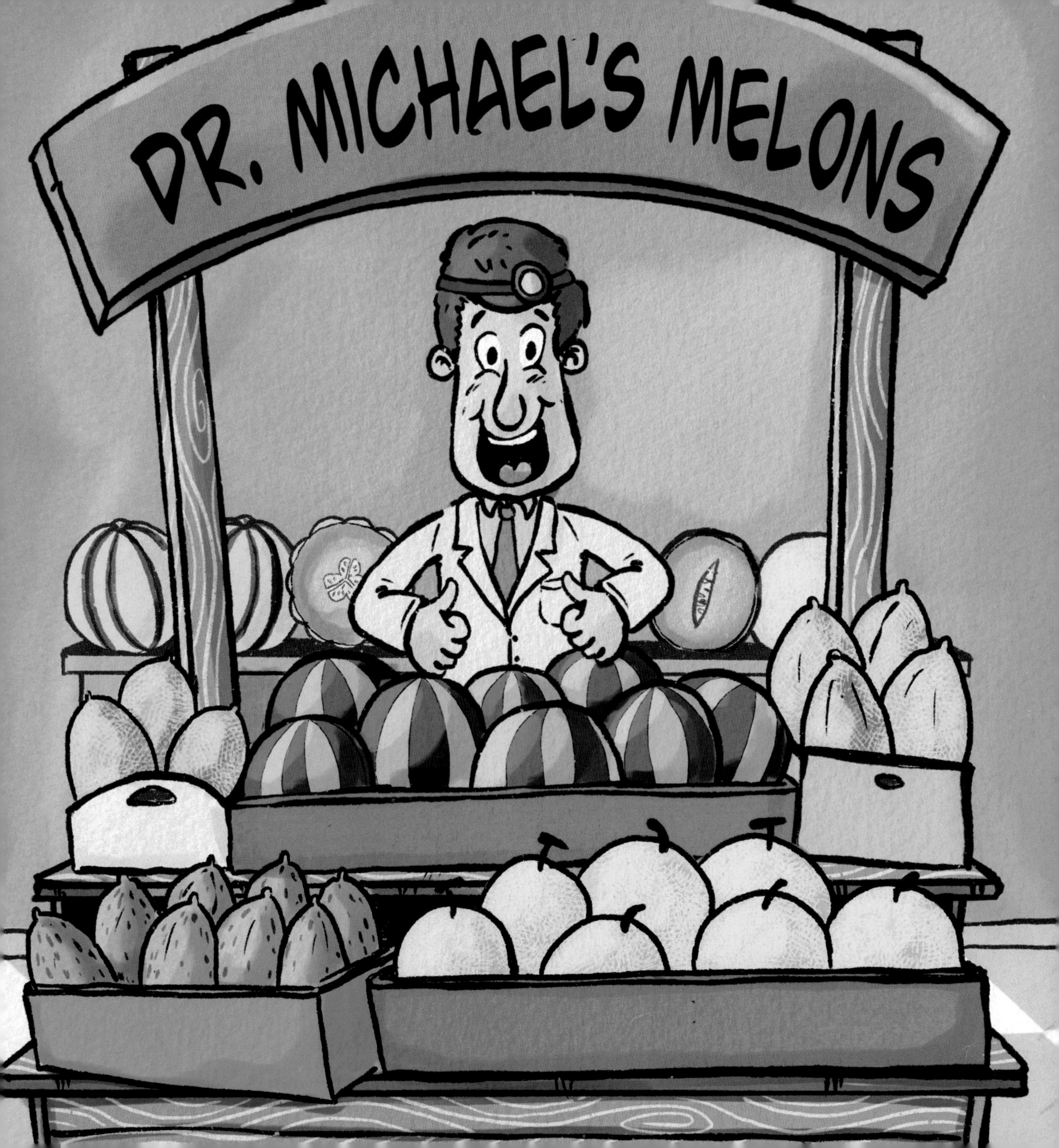
DR. MICHAEL'S MELONS

"It was lovely to chat but we'll be on our way, I'm feeling unsafe with these two on display."

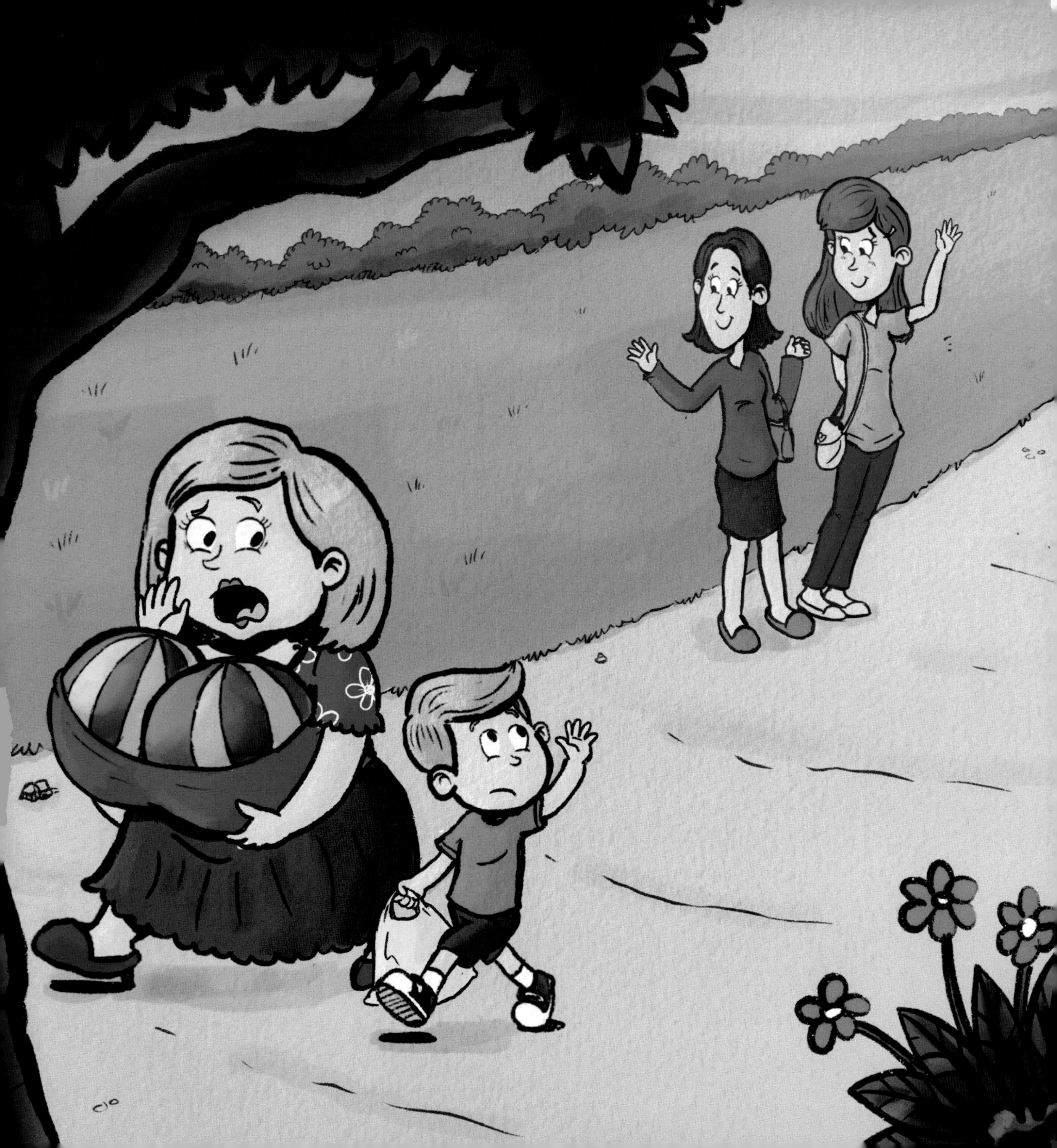

"Has nobody seen massive melons before?"
I said as she squeezed them to fit through
the door.

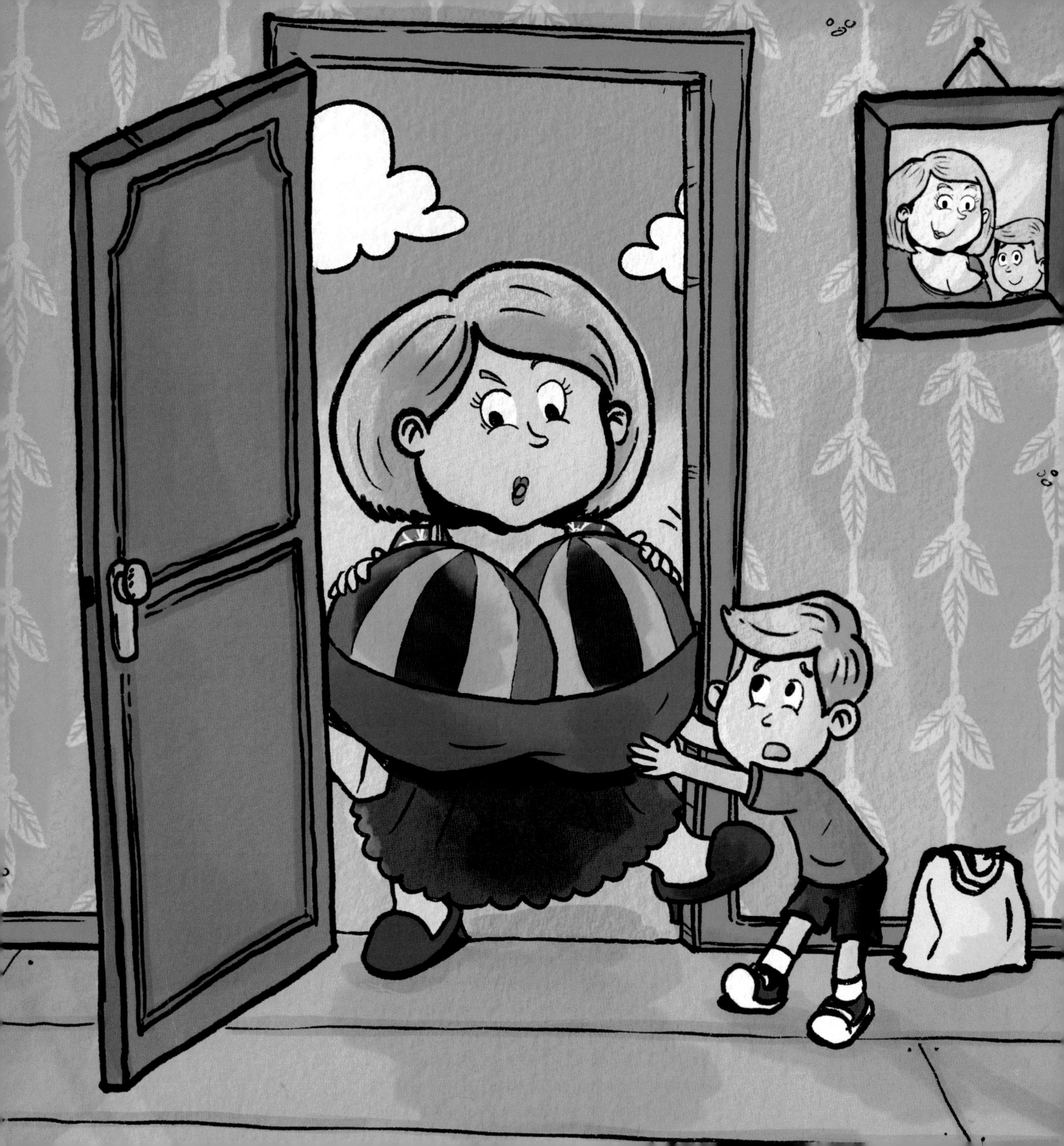

"You're right kid, that's true, but you have to admit, melons this giant are hard to forget."

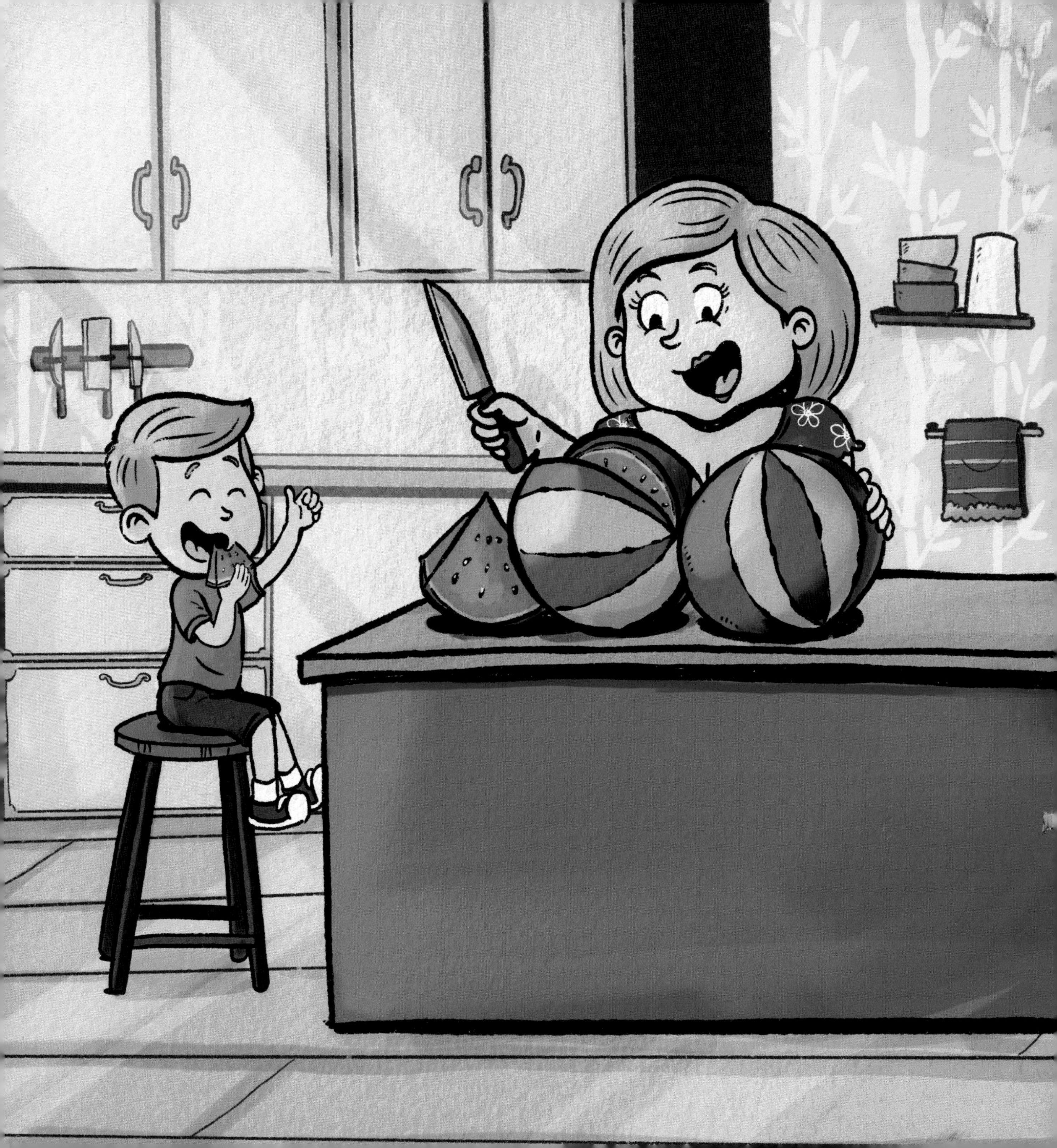

Hey there reader,

Thanks so much for taking the time out of your life to read this brilliant piece of literature... I mean, this silly little book. I hope it made you smile the way it makes me smile. This is my first book EVER, and I'm super excited that at least one person bought it (joking...not joking). If you enjoyed it, it would mean the world to me if you'd leave a review over on Amazon and maybe even share it with a friend or two.

I'd love to stay in touch and keep you updated on my upcoming projects (I've got several in the works). So, go ahead and hit up MamaJC.com and subscribe to my newsletter. I promise... no spammy stuff. You can also come hang out with me on TikTok, Instagram, and Facebook with the handle: @hellomamajc.

Catcha next time,

Mama JC

Manufactured by Amazon.ca
Bolton, ON

23162224R00019